A Journey to Truth

31 Days of Devotion and Prayer

LaShundra S. Smith

A Journey to Truth
Copyright © 2019 by LaShundra S. Smith

ISBN (978-1-7331258-1-9)

Acknowledgements

I would like to take this time to give honor where honor is due, give praise where praise is due. All the glory belongs to the Lord. Lord, thank you for using me as your blueprinted vessel to assist others in finding you and finding your truth. None of this could have been done without your promptings and strength. I am forever grateful. To my mother, Antoinette Modique, thank you for trusting God at his word; and believing that "He gave me to you". Looking to protect me at all times, and knowing that there was a higher calling upon my life. Thank you my wonderful children, Amere', Desiree, Amayah, Aleric, Alijah, A'Lellia, A'Nyra and Fentress Smith Jr. Because of you and the Lord's hand being upon my life, my life is better and forever changed. Thank you for accepting me even when I was not walking with Christ. Thank you for loving me, and expressing your love toward me. Amayah- you played a huge part in the completion of this book. You may not ever know the depths of gratitude and appreciation I have for you. Thank you for your sacrifice in waking with me each morning to seek the Father for direction as I embarked on this journey. I'm waiting with excitement and anticipation to see God use you in a mighty way for his kingdom and glory. To my family, thank you for understanding when I could not be in attendance physically to every event. I love you all and look forward to our next gathering. To my leaders where the work first began, Arch-Bishop Bobby E. Pierson and Pastor Swanderlyn Pierson; thank you taking me in and nursing me back to life; and for planting and watering the seeds within me. Your prayers and guidance means more to me than I could ever express. I appreciate you recognizing God in me, even when I did not recognize it myself. Bishop, the word of the Lord that you spoke over my life during my ordination service March 21, 2016 has begun to manifest! This is the first of many books God has placed within me, and I am grateful that you are able to be a witness, again, of God's glory being revealed. I honor you both. To my current leaders; Apostle Winston Cooper and Leading Lady Jessica Cooper, thank you. Thank you for speaking over my life and watching along with God to be sure I expanded and executed. I am forever grateful to have such awesome leaders that has not only given such wonderful impartations, but also put in the work with me. Thank you, Thank you, and Thank you. I love you all. Grace and peace be multiplied to you all.

Table of Contents

Introduction

"A Journey to Truth" expels all lies of the enemy. This book was written to remind you of God's truth and perception regarding everyday matters. I've included practical steps to take that will ensure a mind change, perception change; and draw you closer to God.

To the unbeliever: My prayer is that you are brought into the marvelous light by entrusting the Spirit filled words upon each page. May you apply the word to your life and watch the transformation begin to take place. May the Lord visit you along this journey and you not miss your divine appointment with Christ. May your reflections reveal the truth of Christ and you accept him as your Lord and Savior.

To the babe in Christ: May each day help you along your way. I pray you believe and receive the words spoken from the Spirit. May your commitment to Christ become richer each day. May every doubt be cancelled and may you become closer to God, knowing and being confident that his words are truth. May you grow in respect to salvation by tasting the kindness of the Lord. (1 Peter 2:2-3)

Day 1
The Pursuit

John 20:29
Isaiah 55:6
Joshua 24:14-15

The first step in this process is to be intentional about pursuing Christ. Whether you are a believer or not, you must first make a choice, choosing not to make a choice is still a choice. You have to make up your mind and say **I choose Christ;** I choose to learn more of him, and I choose this day to serve the one and only true living God. Every day, you hold the decision of a lifetime, which is the decision to serve God Almighty. If you have been serving God for some time now, then you know having a renewed spirit and choosing the Lord is a daily choice. If you have not yet accepted Christ as your Lord and Savior, today is a really good day to make that choice. If you are not sure God exist, today is a really good day to make a conscious decision to seek the Lord while he may be found, seek to learn more of him, and seek to have an encounter with him, for blessed are they that have not seen yet believe.

One way to pursue Christ

Prayer is a conversation between you and God. You can begin speaking to the Lord from a pure heart, being true and transparent with yourself and God. You can tell God anything, and you can ask God any question. God hears and he answers prayers. After you pour out your heart, begin to listen for his voice as he begins to speak to you. God speaks in many different ways. He impresses upon your heart, he speaks with an audible voice, or he speaks through visions. Stay open and listen to what the Lord will say.

Prayer: Father God in the mighty name of Jesus, meet me right where I am today. I choose to serve you; I want to know more of you, and I seek your face. I accept you as my Lord and Savior. Come into my heart and cleanse me again. Thank you for not giving up on me. Thank you for loving me, and I thank you for guiding me, in Jesus' mighty name. Amen.

<u>Day 2</u>
The Love of God

1 John 4:19
John 3:16
1 John 4:7-8
1 Corinthians 13:4-7

The word love has been used loosely for decades. Webster's definition of love is: strong affection for another, attraction based on sexual desire, unselfish, loyal, and benevolent. We have had the wrong idea of what true love really is. The true definition of love exemplifies a perfect love, one that is not boastful, not puffed up, patient, kind, does not envy, not self-seeking, does not dishonor others, is not easily angered, keeps no record of wrongs, does not delight in evil but rejoices with truth always, protects, trusts, hopes, and perseveres. God is love. He loved us so much that he gave his only begotten son to redeem us while we were yet sinners. We love God now because he first loved us. He loved hell out of us, which makes his love perfect. We should display love to all mankind. Love wholeheartedly, love our neighbors as ourselves, and love with an Agape love, not with conditions or restraints. God commanded us to love one another; for love comes from God. Love on someone that you find difficult to love and let the Lord teach you how to love properly.

Ways to show love

Be patient, don't get easily angered
Love unconditional, look past shortcomings and love anyway
Be understanding, don't be quick to judge

Prayer: Father, I come to give you thanks for first loving me. Thank you for giving up your son for my sins. Teach me to love like you love, help me to show the type of love that is pleasing unto you. Give me a special grace to love the unlovable. Help me to love unconditionally and show the love of Christ. May I be the vessel to love your people back to life. May the love I exude, heal and deliver your people, in Jesus' name. Amen.

Day 3
Think About Your Thoughts

Proverbs 23:7
Philippians 4:8
Romans 12:2
2 Corinthians 10:5

Your thoughts are very powerful. If you are not conscious of the thoughts you entertain, they can quickly become your actions. Today, make a conscious decision to think positive. You have had enough negative thoughts for a lifetime. Shift your thinking to a different dimension. Begin to think on things that are true, honest, just, pure, lovely, and of a good report. I know the ins and outs of your daily life may bring about some hardship in remaining positive, but being sure you renew your mind daily with the word of God, will help you become transformed. Your renewed mind causes you to prove what the good, acceptable, and perfect will of God is. Remember, whatever you think in your heart, so are you. Start the day with thinking positively, pay attention to your thoughts, bring every evil thought under subjection to Christ, and be healed, be delivered; and be set free from every bondage of the mind.

Prayer: Lord, continue to stay at the forefront of my mind. Help me to maintain a renewed mind. I know if I keep my mind on you, you will keep me in perfect peace. I'm grateful I am able to think on things that are true, things that are honest, and of a good report. May every vain imagination be broken and scattered. Bind my mind to the mind of Christ, in Jesus' name. Amen.

Day 4
Love The Skin You're In

Psalms 139:14-15
Ephesians 2:10
Philippians 1:6

I know it can be challenging to remain confident in ourselves. You may struggle with being confident in your job, your relationships, your ministry, and even your image, skin, or body. Today take back what the enemy has stolen from you, and begin to believe what God says about you. Choose to let go of all the lies the enemy told you. You are good enough. You are great at what you do. You are not perfect, but you were perfectly crafted by God. Begin to love the skin you're in. Love you for you. You have permission to love yourself. Love the person God has created you to be. Forgive yourself for your shortcomings and be confident that God will perfect what he began in you, until the day of Christ Jesus. Praise God for creating such a wonderful masterpiece. Except it, walk in it, and own it. You are Christ's handiwork. You are fearfully and wonderfully made. His works are marvelous; look at yourself in the mirror, and now, love YOU!

Prayer: Father, forgive me for being the clay attempting to tell the Potter he messed up his work of art. Forgive me for not accepting myself the way you created me. I thank you for revealing my worth. I thank you for your marvelous works. I praise you because I am fearfully and wonderfully made. Let me hold fast to your truth about me, for you created me for your works. Thank you for boosting my self-esteem and my confidence in Jesus' name I pray. Amen.

Day 5
Trust the Lord

Proverbs 3:5-6
Psalm 9:10
Psalms 20:7
Psalm 118:8
Pray Romans 15:13

No matter what comes your way today, choose to believe God. No matter the circumstances, no matter your issues, still choose to believe God. Sometimes the wiles of the world will cause you to believe what you see. Put and maintain your trust in the Lord. Make a conscious effort to trust in the Lord with all your heart, and lean not unto your own understanding, in all your ways acknowledge him, and he will direct your path. If you are trusting in the Lord to do something for you, don't give up hope. Don't try to figure out how God will do it; just trust that he can and he will. Even if an extended amount of time has passed, hold on to your trust in the Lord. This can be a challenging task, but you should trust God because he is God and does not exhibit the same character as man. God cannot and will not fail you. The more you begin to know God, truly learn who is, you will trust in him. Don't trust more in your job, cars, or friends, but put all of your trust in the most-high God.

Prayer: Lord thank you for being God. Thank you for being faithful when I was faithless. Thank you for being trustworthy. I put my trust in no one or nothing but you. Help my unbelief. Heal my trust issues that stemmed from man, causing me to not trust you with my whole heart. No matter what I see, I trust you because you are not a man that shall lie, nor the son of man that shall repent. Teach me to trust you wholeheartedly. I will not depend upon my own understanding but I lean upon you. I acknowledge you and I expect you to direct my path. I love you and I honor your holy name. Amen.

<u>Day 6</u>
Focus On Christ

Philippians 3:13-14
Proverbs 4:25-26
Hebrews 12:1

Keep your focus on Christ! This has proven to be quite a task. In order to remain focused on anything, there needs to be a certain level of commitment. Commit to focus on what God has set before you. Don't look around, don't look down, and don't look back, but look forward. Look up to the author and finisher of your faith. Keep going. Don't give up, and don't lose hope. You have a great crowd of witnesses cheering you on. He called you out of the boat. Now, walk straightway, not looking to the left or right, but look unto God, and let him establish your way!

Prayer: Lord Jesus, help me to remain focused on the things you have called me to accomplish. Help me to remain faithful to the things I have started. Forgive me for losing my vigor, my fire, my vision, and my focus. Refine my lenses and let me see through your lenses. I look to you and I keep my eyes on you. Do not let the storms of life overwhelm me. I bind every distraction that has come to take my focus. Lord, thank you for establishing my way in Jesus' name, I pray. Amen.

Day 7
You Are Forgiven

1 John 1:9
Colossians 1:13-14
Psalms 103:10-12
Matthew 6:14-15

Today is the day to accept your forgiveness from the Lord, your God. Let go of past mistakes and iniquities, and remember them no more. You don't have to wear disappointment and shame any more. You serve an awesome God. He is faithful to forgive us when we ask. Come clean with God and be transparent with him. Confess your sins and ask for forgiveness. You were redeemed by his precious blood. He has not dealt with you according to your sins, which demonstrates how merciful he is. Begin to show the same mercy and forgiveness towards those that have wronged you. When you pray and ask God for forgiveness, be sure to forgive others. In order to receive forgiveness, you must forgive. Forgive the individual that hurt you, lied on you, betrayed you, talked about you, and etc. Free yourself. Be healed, be free, and be made whole. He has brought you out of the darkness into his marvelous light. He has conveyed us into the kingdom of his son, who has redeemed us by his blood. Be forgiven.

Prayer: Lord God, I thank you for your redemptive power. I thank you for being just and faithful to forgive my transgressions. I am forgiven and I am free. I will no longer wear the shame of my past. I will no longer let my past mistakes keep me from fully walking into my destiny. I take off the rags of dishonor, shame, and un-forgiveness. I put on the righteousness of Christ, the garments of praise, and the crown of righteousness. I receive your forgiveness by faith, just as I forgave others by faith. Amen.

Day 8
Worship Me

John 4:24
Psalms 99:5
Isaiah 29:13

Do you know what true worship is or what true worship looks like? Are you a worshiper? To worship God is to express a genuine honor in reverence to our holy God. To worship the Lord our God is to stand in truth, your truth, exuding the love from your heart, with a special expression to our King. Think about a difficult time you endured in the past. God brought you out didn't he? Has he ever done anything amazing for you or your family and friends? He deserves our worship and honor. Those who worship him must worship him in spirit and truth. It should be an easy thing to offer up praise from your lips unto the Lord. It should be automatic to offer up wave offerings, lifting of your voice or lifting of your hands. Sadly, not all people are able to offer God true worship. Lift up his name, bow before his feet, and worship at his footstool, for he is holy. You come into a true space of worship when you can identify and acknowledge your shortcomings. Your walk may not have been perfect, but God still chose you. He delivered you, and he saved you. This makes it easier to worship God. You will be humble enough, thankful enough, and excited to bow down and worship the Lord.

Prayer: Father God, let me not only use my lips to honor you, but let my heart be close to you. I shall worship you in spirit and truth. I love you. I lift you up, and I magnify your holy name. Let the posture of my heart be pleasing and give glory to you. I bless you in Jesus' name. I shall worship you with my life in daily living. Create in me a clean heart and a right spirit. I desire the right spirit to worship you with a pure heart. Let my worship be pure unto you. In Jesus' name. Amen.

Day 9

Be Courageous

Deuteronomy 31:6
2 Timothy 1:7
Ephesians 6:10
Psalms 56:3-4

Today is the day that you should step out of the box! Make a move, press forward, and take the first step to do whatever it is you have always wanted to do. That business venture has been waiting, and your God ordained ministry has been waiting long enough. If God be for you, who could be against you? Let nothing hold you back any longer. Don't be afraid because God did not give you a spirit of fear, but of power, love, and a sound mind. Write that book, what are you afraid of? God has commanded that you walk into your wealthy place; walk into your land that's flowing with milk and honey. Do not be afraid; instead, be strong and of good courage. Your new, prosperous destiny awaits you!

Prayer: Father God, in the name of Jesus, grant me the courage needed to overtake the land that you have given to me to possess. Let me walk boldly and fearlessly into my destiny. I know that you are with me; therefore, I pay no attention to any adversary I may face. What shall they do unto me? I will do all that you command. I will be strong because I am strong in the power of your might. I am courageous and I will start and finish all that you have called me to do. Thank you for your strength, might, and courage, in Jesus' name. Amen.

Day 10
Faithfulness

1 Corinthians 4:2
Deuteronomy 7:9
Numbers 23:19
Matthew 25:23

There are many areas in your life that require your faithfulness. There can be many things vying for your immediate attention. To be faithful is to be loyal, constant, and steadfast. Have you exhibited faithfulness to your household, your job, your spouse? God requires us to be faithful and good stewards over everything he has entrusted to us. Just as you require your spouse to be faithful to you, God wants the same thing. He said if you are faithful over a few things he will make you ruler over much. God has shown us that whenever you commit yourself to something or someone, it is important to complete the task. Jesus was an example to faithfulness because he was faithful to the cross. The Lord is faithful even when we are faithless and his mercies are renewed daily. Connect with your church family and continue to remain faithful to your duties. When you are faithful in God's works he is faithful in yours. He is not a man that he shall lie, or the son of man that he shall repent.

Prayer: Lord I come to you, asking that you make me more faithful. Make me faithful in every area of my life. I thank you for remaining faithful to me even when I was not faithful. I bless your holy name for your faithfulness to me. Make me ruler over much; make me a faithful steward. Thank you for doing it Lord. Amen.

Day 11
Walking In Faith

2 Corinthians 5:7
Mark 11:42
John 11:40
Hebrews 11:6

God has given each of us a measure of faith. To have faith is to cancel out unbelief. You are able to pray and ask God for anything. Ask God and believe he will do it, and it will be yours. God is the creator of all things, so how much more should we put full trust in him? Have faith without unbelief, and do not waver, because you never wonder if your house key will unlock your door from one day to the next. Your faith is your key to unlocking Gods favor and blessings upon you and your household. Use your key daily.

Prayer: Father God, thank you for the faith you have given me. Activate my faith to be used on another level. Lord, begin to increase my faith even now. I know it is impossible to please you without faith. I choose to have faith to please you so that your glory may manifest in my life. I believe that anytime I come to you in prayer, it shall be done. I will walk by faith and not by sight. Thank you for being faithful and dependable. Thank you for loving me. Amen.

Day 12
Be Made Whole

John 5:6
Jeremiah 30:17
3 John 1:2
1 Thessalonians 5:23

To be whole is to be all, entire, unbroken, intact, undamaged, and one piece. We go through life as if we are whole when in actuality; we have pieces of ourselves in many places. Also, when you give people pieces of you, you become incomplete. If you are broken, God has to restore you back to good health. God is requiring you to be whole, and you also have a choice in the matter. Don't sit around any longer in bitterness, anger, hurt, un-forgiveness, or even disappointments. Now is the time to claim your healing. God wishes that you prosper even as your soul prospers. Begin to depend on the Lord to restore you, heal you, and mend the hurt and pain. Joy and laughter is your portion. God will sanctify you completely.

Prayer: Lord I give my entire being to you. Restore my soul, heal my heart and deliver me. I choose to be made whole. I walk in my victory. Remove the reproach of my past. Heal my wounds. I thank you that I am whole. Thank you for your faithfulness. I thank you that I don't have to live my life in pieces; I can live a whole, prosperous, loving, joyous, and peaceful life. Thank you for your loving kindness in Jesus' name, Amen.

Day 13
Yearning for Christ

Matthew 5:6
Psalms 63:1
Psalms 42:1-2

Often, we desire things that are offered by the world. These things may include the newest cars, the latest designer bags, hottest wardrobe, and admirable relationships. We as kingdom citizens should yearn for the deeper things of God. We should desire a closer more intimate relationship with him. There has to be a longing within our souls for Christ. When you hunger and thirst after righteousness you shall be filled. Begin to seek God earnestly and wholeheartedly. Effectively cry out to the Lord, your savior. Crave his attention and you shall be blessed.

Prayer: Father God, let me not desire the things of this world more than I desire you. Let me crave for more of you and less of me. Lord I am hungry for more of your love, wisdom, and power. I need you in my life. Begin to increase my spiritual appetite. I hunger and thirst after you. I want a deeper and closer relationship with you. Draw me near oh Lord, and hear my prayer. I love you and I seek you in Jesus' name. Amen.

Day 14
My Grace is Sufficient

2 Corinthians 12:9
Ephesians 2:8-9
Hebrews 4:16

To feel you are not strong enough to handle certain situations, couldn't be further from the truth. God's grace is all you need to start a task and complete a task. When you are weak he is made strong. His power is perfected during your weak moments. God's grace is sufficient. Be grateful you were saved by his grace. God is all-knowing and he knew you would be too weak to carry through. You are not powerful enough to save yourself. Because of his loving kindness towards you, he saved you. Call on God with confidence, knowing his grace will sustain you.

Prayer: Lord thank you for your saving grace towards me. I praise you because when I am weak, you make me strong. I am able to come boldly before you to receive help in my time of need. I know that your grace is sufficient for me, and I thank you for providing the grace needed to finish this race. May you be glorified. Amen.

Day 15

Be Resilient

Ephesians 6:10-11
James 1:2-4
Exodus 14:13-14

Although there are many trials you may face, do not fear. "Be resilient, for I have overcome the world," says the Lord. No matter what stumbling block you've encountered, be strong in the power of his might. Stand still, bounce back, be tough, and withstand the enemy's schemes, by putting on the whole armor of God. When you are faced with many difficulties, count it all joy knowing the Lord your God will help you endure until the end.

Prayer: Lord I honor your name. I praise you for you are greatly to be praised. I thank you for making me tough, resilient, and having a word I can stand on. Your word is sure and your word is true. I trust in the power of your might. I put on the whole armor of God so that I am able to withstand the attacks of the enemy. Thank you for your protection, grace, and favor. Amen.

Day 16
No More Shame

Isaiah 54:4
Romans 10:11
Psalms 25:3

We know all things work together for the good of those who love the Lord and are called according to his purpose. The bible emphasizes that all things work together, not some things. Today, let go of your shameful past. Past mistakes, downfalls, and decisions shall not have you feeling ashamed any more. Scripture declares whoever believes in God will not be disappointed. Once you decide to embrace your healing, do not be ashamed, hold your head up high, and choose freedom. You are no longer bound by your past. You shall forget the shame of your youth and the reproach of your widowhood.

Prayer: Lord thank you for removing my shameful past. Thank you for turning my mourning into joy. Thank you for removing the reproach from my head. Help me to keep my head held high and refuse to have shame upon my shoulders. I've accepted the good that has come from my past. Thank you for justifying a sinner like me. You are truly worthy to be praised. Thank you for being a forgiving God. Amen.

Day 17
Stay Persistent

Luke 18:1-8
Galatians 6:9
1 Corinthians 15:58
Philippians 1:6

Some things may come easy or you may have to work a little harder to achieve. All in all, persevere, remain focused, and stay persistent. You will accomplish your goals. Do not give up, do not get tired, and do not grow weary. For in due season, you will reap if you do not faint. Whether it is in life or ministry, know that he who began a good work in you will bring it to completion, keep going.

Prayer: Father God in the name of Jesus, I thank you for giving me the strength to be persistent. Continue to help me stay the course. I know that you will perfect what you have started within me. Help me to remain steadfast, unmovable and always abounding in your work. I know I will reap my harvest if I do not faint. I will not lose hope; I will persevere; I will push through, and keep going. Help me to remain focused, in Jesus' name. Amen.

Day 18
Single Mindedness

James 1:8
Romans 12:2
James 4:8
Matthew 6:24

Being indecisive is choosing to be double minded. James points out in scripture; being double minded creates an environment of instability. It's impossible for you to have any clarity while being double minded. Put on the mind of Christ by renewing your mind with scripture, washing daily. Once you make up your mind to serve Christ, you'll be able to draw near to God, get cleansed and be of a sound mind. Be whole, where your mind and spirit or one, and not torn.

Prayer: Father I thank you for your word. I thank you for your loving kindness towards me. I put on the mind of Christ so that I can be single minded. Bind my mind to the mind of Christ. Keep me rooted in pleasuring you. I am stable and whole. I will not be tossed to-and-fro, because I am unshakable, unmovable, and always abounding in the works of the Lord. Thank you for keeping me with a sound mind. I praise your name for you are holy and faithful. Amen.

Day 19

Give Your Cares to Me

Matthew 11:28
1 Peter 5:7
Philippians 4:6

The cares of tomorrow, the weight of the world and the anxiety of the unknown are not your portion. All that labor and are heavy laden should go straight to God. Give him every burden, every issue, every concern, and every worry. Lay it at his feet and leave it there. He's waiting to give you the rest you seek. Whatever it is that you are concerned about, God is also concerned about. Give it to him he's more equipped to hold it all.

Prayer: Lord, I come to you at the foot of your throne, releasing the cares of this world to you. Lord I cast all of my cares upon you, for I know that you care for me. You told me if I was heavy laden to come to you, so I come to you seeking my rest. I know your burden is easy and your yoke is light. I thank you for perfecting those things that concern me. I thank you for your peace that surpasses all understanding. I thank you for being mindful of me. Amen.

Day 20
Command Your Angels

Psalms 91:11
Psalms 103:20
Hebrews 1:14
Psalms 34:7
Exodus 23:20

 The Lord has given his angels charge over you, to help you along the way. They will keep you from stumbling or falling. They await instructions from you daily. Command your angels to go to work on your behalf. Using the word of God, begin to declare and decree a thing, then send your angles out, and watch God perform his word. You have angels of protection, provision, and direction. Your angels are ministering spirits that minister unto you according to your needs; so command your angels to perform the will of God for your life.

Prayer: Father God in the name of Jesus, thank you for assigning angels over my life. I thank you for the authority in commanding my angels to go to work on my behalf. Thank you for being mindful of me. I'm grateful to have ministering spirits to be there for me, to guard me, and to help me. They are listening for your words to be obedient unto them, so I thank you for your word, in Jesus' name. Amen.

Day 21
Be Encouraged

Psalms 16:8
Jeremiah 29:11
Romans 8:31

No matter what circumstance you face, no matter what you go through, no matter what the situation looks like, be sure you stay encouraged. When things do not seem to be going your way, when it seems like no one is on your side, be encouraged. Know that if God be for you, it's better than the whole world against you. Press forward, be on guard, stand firm in your faith, be courageous, and be strong.

Prayer: Lord I encourage myself, knowing that you are on my side. Having you on my side is better than the whole world against me. I'm thankful that you are my helper, strength, and a very present help in the time of need. No matter what it looks like, I choose to stay encouraged, standing and believing in your word. Amen.

Day 22
Repent

2 Chronicles 7:14
1 John 1:9
Acts 3:19
Proverbs 1:23

To repent is to change your mind and turn away from the sin. You have to begin to change the way you perceive the very thing you are engaged in. Also, you must turn from it and never do it again. This is where you can begin to turn to God, seek his face and be refreshed. True repentance is expressed from your heart and not your lips. Once you ask God for forgiveness, he is faithful and just to forgive you. Be sure to live a fully repentant life, so that you are continually purified from all unrighteousness.

Prayer: Father God, I ask that you continue to forgive me for anything I have thought, said, or done that was displeasing to you. Forgive me for all things I have committed and omitted. I thank you for your faithfulness to forgive. I receive your forgiveness by faith. Keep me righteous, keep my feet in your will, keep my mind on you, and keep my heart turned towards you. Thank you for your refreshing in Jesus' name. Amen.

Day 23
Write the Vision

Habakkuk 2:2- 3
Psalms 5:3
Matthew 21:22

What plans, dreams, visions, or aspirations do you have? Have you written them down or created a vision board? Whatever is on your heart to accomplish, accomplish it. Start by writing the vision as you see it. Sit the vision in a place where you can see it and you'll begin to run to complete it. Make it plain and succeed. Anything you ask in prayer, believing, you will receive.

Prayer: Lord, give me your vision for my life. Let me see my world, life and future through your eyes. Place your perfect desires for me upon my heart. Align my life according to your will. Thank you for answering my prayers; thank you for giving me the vision to write. I thank you for being God. Amen.

Day 24
Be Thankful

1 Thessalonians 5:18
Colossians 3:17
Philippians 4:6
Psalms 106:1
Hebrews 12:28-29

No matter the day, month, or year, you should be thankful! No matter the test, trial, circumstance, or situation, be thankful to the Lord, for this is his perfect will. In every area of your life, give thanks, for the Lord is good and his love endures forever. Thank God for this day. Thank God for all the things you have and your praise will be rich. When things aren't going your way or the way you expected them to go, give thanks to God anyway! His Kingdom cannot be shaken, so be thankful and worship the Lord with reverence and awe.

Prayer: Lord I come to give you thanks today. I have not told you enough, and I know I can never tell you enough because that's just how good and merciful you have been to me. Thank you for your everlasting love. Thank you for your blood and for blessing me to see this day. This is the day you made and I will be glad in it. Lord you are good and I reverence you. Thank you for being God. I love you, praise you, and adore you in Jesus' name. Amen.

Day 25
Removing Idols

Deuteronomy 5:6
Matthew 6:24
1 John 5:21
Colossians 3:5
Jonah 2:8
Leviticus 19:4

An idol is an image or representation of a god, used as an object of worship, or a person or thing that is greatly admired, loved, or revered. This can include people, places, things, objects, etc. Begin to examine your life and daily routines. Take note of any idols you have in any area of your life. Anything that has caused you to place God on the back burner is an idol. Begin to pinpoint these things and pull down their altars, demolish the pedestals, and let God begin to rein in their place. Allow God to rein in every area of your life.

Prayer: Father God in the mighty name of Jesus, forgive me for placing false gods before you. Forgive me for putting my job, family, and myself before you. Purify my heart and pull down every idle god. Remove their altars from my heart. You are my God, take your place and have your way in my life. I put you first; I love you and adore you. You are my King forever. Amen.

Day 26
Know the Truth

John 8:31-32
John 1:17
John 14:6
John 16:13
Psalms 119:160
Psalms 25:5
Proverbs 12:22

By following Jesus' commandments, laws, and precepts, you are allowing Christ to guide and teach you. Jesus said, "*You will know the truth and the truth will make you free*." You do not have to be bound. Once you learn the truth you are free from bondages. Jesus is the way the truth and the life. Disregard every lie, false hope, deceptive word, and seek God for the truth regarding your future and his will.

Prayer: Lord, open my eyes to your truth. Remove every lie of the enemy. Let me stand firm on your words as they are truth and life. I thank you for your words and for speaking over my life. I thank you for your word making me free. I thank you for being my God and savior. Your truth guides and teaches me. I put my hope in you. Amen.

Day 27
Guard Your Gates

Luke 11:34-35
Proverbs 4:23
Luke 6:45
Psalm 141:3

It is so important to guard what you see, hear, and speak. Guarding your gates is your responsibility. Often, we are too lackadaisical regarding the types of things we watch, read, listen to, or say. Begin to guard your heart because out of it flows the issues of life. Be sure to watch and read things that radiate light, because your body will be filled with whatever you allow through your gates. Be sure it is not darkness that enters in.

Prayer: Lord, consume me with your righteousness. Help me guard my ear gates, eye gates, and mouth gate. O' Lord, set a guard over my mouth. Continue to lead me into your marvelous light. Let me watch, read, and see only things you intend for me. May I hear and adhere to only your voice; may my lips be touched by you, so that I do not transgress against you. Lord, I thank you for keeping guard over my gates, in Jesus' name. Amen.

Day 28
I'm Always There

Deuteronomy 31:6
Isaiah 41:10
Romans 8:38-39
Psalms 23:4

No matter what you need or how you feel, the Lord your God is right there by your side. He has made a promise to be with you, even until the end of the world. There is no need to fear the unknown because we serve an all-knowing God. Did he not say to be strong and courageous and to fear not? I don't care what you may face, the Lord will strengthen you.

Prayer: I thank you for always being there for me and not forsaking me. I will not be afraid and shall be strong with your strength. I shall move forward, knowing that you are always there for me and you walk beside me. In that alone, I am comforted in Jesus' name. Amen.

Day 29
Total Surrender

Galatians 2:20
James 4:7
Jeremiah 10:23
Romans 8:1-2
Luke 9 1:23-24
Job 11:13-20

Did you know that your life is not your own? You were bought with a price. The precious blood of Jesus was shed for your salvation. God wants you totally surrendered. He wants you to stretch your arms up high and posture your heart towards him. Completely surrender to him with no partiality, not halfway, or going back. Present your body a living sacrifice. If you submit yourself to God the devil shall flee from you. Don't wait another day, now is the time. Lay it all at his holy feet. Surrender your mind, heart, body, and soul to Christ.

Prayer: Father God, in the name of Jesus, please forgive me for holding out on you. Forgive me for not being fully committed and totally surrendered to you. Lord I love you. I surrender myself and relinquish all of my desires unto you. I will wait for your instructions and obey them. I'll be your eyes, ears, mouth, feet, and hands in the earth. My heart is available for you to reign over my life. I submit to the vocation. Lord thank you for choosing me in Jesus' name. Amen.

Day 30
Be Obedient

John 15:14
Luke 11:28
1 Samuel 15:22
James 1 verse 22
John 14:23
Proverbs 10:17
Isaiah 1:19

What was the last thing God told you to do? Have you done it? Most times, we offer up a sacrifice unto God in lieu of doing what he has asked. The Lord requires your obedience. If you are willing and obedient God promises you will eat the good of the land. You are blessed when you hear the word of the Lord and obey it. Don't be deceived. Once you hear the word you must also do what he says. Now is the time to revisit what the Lord's last instruction to you was, and obey it, so you may be blessed and become a friend of Jesus.

Prayer: Lord, let me remain obedient to your will. I thank you for your mercy and grace. I thank you for being patient with me when I was disobedient. Help me to move quickly and adhere to your word. Keep me focused and give me a heart that wants to please you in Jesus' name. Amen.

Day 31
Pure In Heart

2 Timothy 2:21
Matthew 8:5
Philippians 4:8
Proverbs 16:2
Psalms 51:10
Psalms 119:9

Do you ever think about the reason behind your actions or thoughts? What was the real reason for extending an extra hand or befriending someone? Examine your heart. Be sure there is no hate, offence or grudges in your heart. You may think your ways are pure, but your motives are weighed by the Lord. Begin to ask the Lord to create in you a clean heart and renew a right spirit within you. In order for the Lord to be able to use you for a special purpose, you must first be cleansed. Blessed are those who are with a pure heart for they shall see God.

Prayer: Lord, purify my heart. Begin to remove all unclean things from my heart. Create in me a clean heart and renew a right spirit within me. Make me worthy for your special use because I want to see you. Lord, I choose to live according to your word so that I can stay on the path of purity. Cleanse me, wash me, and make me new. In Jesus' name, Amen.

www.ingramcontent.com/pod-product-compliance
Lightning Source LLC
Chambersburg PA
CBHW070750050426
42449CB00010B/2412